T0413519

purpose size. Use smaller rubber bands like size 16 to bind y small circles.

thetic Sinew is also used. To make very regular circles, d fabric around dried beans or marbles. Designs can also bound with chopsticks or sewn with thread. Shibori designs be bound around a 24" length of 2" to 4" diameter PVC pipe.

ms to Mark Fabric - For some designs, guideline marks need be made on fabric. Use a pencil, piece of chalk or a special rker which makes lines that later wash out. Paper, scissors a ruler may also be needed.

tional Equipment. A dyeing pad or rack can keep dye colors m pooling and mixing under the garments. Use paper tow- or old newspapers with large groups. For small projects, an old plastic dish rack with the tray underneath to catch ess dye. Do not re-use the excess, as it is no longer 'active'. thetic Sinew is preferred by some over rubber bands, as the lines are sharper, and more complex and precise designs possible.

asuring cups & spoons, funnel
duran hand cleaner!

d Garment following each project instructions. Wet garment h plain water before binding to make a sharper design.

ak Garment in Soda Ash Fixer Solution. Soda Ash is mildly ustic, so wear gloves and protect eyes. Wear a dust mask to oid breathing Soda Ash powders. 1 cup per gallon of water es brighter colors but could be too harsh for delicate fabric delicate skin. Use lower concentrations when working with ildren and delicate fabrics, especially silk.

x Dyes - To dissolve dye completely, so you don't end up with eckles', paste it up (mash up with the back of a spoon and a le water) first in another container. Dissolve the Urea in a le hot water, then add some cold water to make 8 oz. of tepid ter. Add this water slowly to the dye powder while mashing with a spoon to make a paste. Gradually add the rest of the ea water while stirring. Use a funnel to fill squeeze bottles. ding a little plain salt to the mix can help yield darker colors, sp per 8 oz of dye mixture. Add last, as salt inhibits the dye ssolving.

epare Dyeing Area. The key to a neat, streamlined experi- ce with dye is to set up your work place ahead of time. Cover ble with plastic and wear a plastic apron. For multi-color proj- ts, make a dyeing pad. Place a piece of plastic wrap on table, en fold 10 paper towels into quarters and place on wrap in me shape as tied garment. The paper towels will act as blot-

ters to keep colors from becoming muddy. Have extra folded paper towels ready when you turn garment over to dye reverse side. If you are dyeing a project all one color or 2 colors to be mixed together, use a shallow plastic tub or bucket.

Apply Dye - Be sure to follow instructions for each project. Be sure to apply dye down into folds if you want saturated color or are making a shaped design. If you want more white show- ing, apply dye on top of folds only. Using a tiny bit of thickener will give crisper lines as it keeps the dye from bleeding into the white or other colors.

Set & Rinse. Remove garment from dyeing pad, wrap in plastic wrap to keep damp (or put in a zip-lock baggie or cover with a plastic tarp). Let set for 4 to 24 hours to allow dye to fix in fibers. Longer setting time produces deeper colors, especially for Turquoise. Rinse in several changes of warm water, remov- ing rubber bands partway through rinsing process. TIP: If you can, rinsing in running water during and after untying is the best technique.

To Remove All Remaining Loose Dye, wash with HOT water and Synthrapol detergent, 1/4 cup per washing machine load. Have machine prefilled and add the garments right out of the rinse. Never stack wet garments on each other. Machine or line dry.

Easy Steps to Tie-Dye - *Have Fun!*

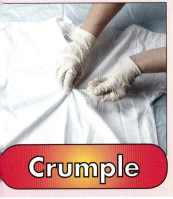

Crumple

Fold

or Tie

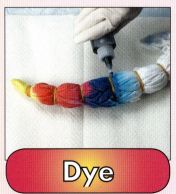

Dye

Crumple-Dye

Blue & White Crumple - Blue dye

1. Push the shirt into crumples with your fingertips.

2. Apply dye in squiggles with spout applicator bottle.

Crumple-dyeing is an easy way to dye fabric with subtl color changes and interesting visual texture. It is also the easies technique and a great place to start. After soaking shirt in fixe spread on table and crumple with fingers into a flat pancak shape. Place in a plastic tub or flat glass baking dish. Apply dy with applicator in an all over squiggle motion. Turn shirt ove keeping crumples and apply dye on back in same way. Place shi on table, flatten and crumple bringing areas without dye to to Dilute dye remaining in applicator bottle by refilling bottle wit water and repeat crumple-dye process. Let set and rinse.

To get even more interesting effects, dye a second time with different color and a third time with a mixture of 2 colors or wit diluted dye. Or use 3 different colors of dye.

An interesting variation is achieved by shaking on dye. Do no cut off tip of applicator spout. A small opening is necessary fo this technique. Crumple fabric as usual and then apply dye b holding bottle in a slanted position and shaking on dye.

Yellow & Orange Crumple - Yellow and Orange dye Dye Yellow, then Orange and diluted Orange.

Yellow & Green Crumple - Yellow, Green and Turquoise dye Dye Yellow, then Turquoise and diluted Turquoise.

A simple technique… dazzling results!
crumple-dyed garments are filled with brilliant
color. Add fun to your wardrobe. It's fast and easy.

Speckle Effect. Hold dye bottle on diagonal and shake on dye, as though you were salting shirt with color. Open and crumple shirt several times until you have desired effect.

Pink & Orange Speckle
Fuchsia and Orange dye
Dye with diluted Fuchsia
and then diluted Orange.

lue & Purple - Blue, Turquoise and Purple dye
pen and re-crumple shirt between each color application.

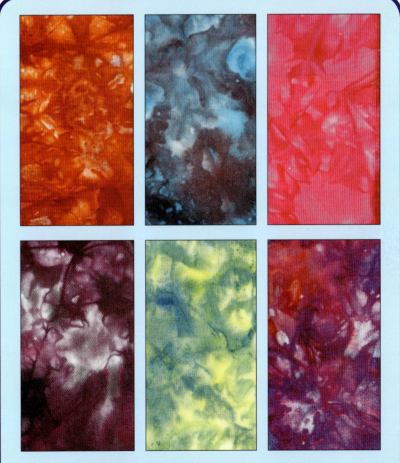

Quilter's Blocks - Assorted dyes
Crumple fabric. Dye with one color, then add diluted color.
Or dye with several colors for the desired effect.

Sunbursts & Circles

Rainbow Sunburst - Fuchsia, Yellow and Turquoise dye

Yellow & Orange Sunburst - Fuchsia, Yellow and Turquoise dye
Dye Yellow down folds and then dye Orange on edges.

1. Pinch center of shirt and bind with a rubber band about 2" down. TIP: Center is on a line with bottom of armholes, not at actual center of shirt.

2. Bind shirt at 2" intervals.

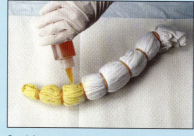

3. After soaking in fixer, apply Yellow dye on tip of shirt and next section.

4. Apply Fuchsia dye on second, third and fourth sections. Then apply Turquoise dye on fourth, fifth and sixth sections. Continue layering colors to make Orange, Green and Purple.

Examples of tie-dyed circles can be found in many cultures including those of Africa, India and Japan. Some of the oldest tie-dyes are done in Africa using this same method. In Japan designs were made of hundreds of tiny circles which were bound with thread around separate grains of rice!

Sunbursts & Circle

are simple to create using very traditional tie-dye technique. Pinch up 1" to 2" of fabric and bind it tightly with a rubber band. Placing several rubber bands at 1" to 2" intervals will create a sunburst design. Placing just one rubber band will make a circle. To make a very regular circle place a small round object like a dried bean in fabric, pinch and then bind. A design can be made with one or many circles.

Stained Glass Sunburst Fold

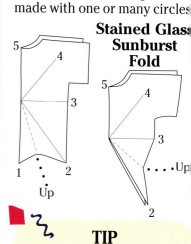

This unusual sunburst is folded into a long triangle before binding.

. Soak shirt in fixer solution. old in half lengthwise.

2. Draw light lines with pencil or disappearing ink. Fold a long triangle by bringing line 1 to line 2 and creasing on dotted line. Repeat 3 more times on the other lines.

. Bind with 4 rubber bands.

tained Glass Sunburst - Yellow, Fuchsia, Turquoise, Black dye fter soaking in fixer solution, dye tip and first section part Yellow and part uchsia. Dye last 2 sections alternately Turquoise, Fuchsia and Yellow. Be sure o inject dye down into folds. After last rubber band, apply Turquoise for about ' and then apply Black dye to rest of shirt. Using an applicator sponge, apply lack just to edges of folds on Rainbow colored part of shirt.

This shirt has layered colors dyed first Red then Turquoise. It is a classic tie-dye method with smooth all-over color that requires no hot water.

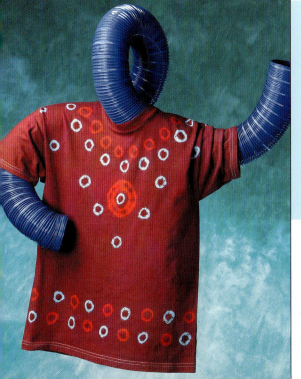

1. Mark shirt with 9 dots evenly spaced about 3" from collar. Mark 2 rows of evenly spaced dots 3" up and 5" up from hem.

2. Place a bean under each dot and bind with a rubber band.

India Style Circles - Red, Blue and Turquoise dye, Dried beans
Bind shirt as marked, soak in fixer. Mix one bottle of Red dye and place in a tub or bowl. Add 2 tablespoons of salt and 3 cups of warm water. Move shirt around in dye for 10 minutes for solid color. Leave in dye for one hour stirring occasionally. Remove rubber bands and beans, rinse thoroughly and wring dry. The shirt will be Red with White circles. Mark and bind Red circle pattern. Bind 2 spaced rubber bands around central circle. Wet shirt with fixer then dye with Turquoise using same method. Remove all rubber bands, rinse and wash.

Rainbow Swirl - Fuchsia, Yellow and Turquoise dye

The Swirl is a popular design that can be done with many variations. The basic technique is simple. Press down at center of fabric and twist until all fabric is swirled into a flat pancake shape. Bind with big rubber bands crossing them in center so shape is divided into wedges. This design can be varied in many ways depending on how colors are applied to wedges.

1. Place shirt flat and pinch a bit of fabric at center. Center is on a line with bottom of armholes, not at actual center of shirt.

2. Pressing down, wind shirt into a flat swirl. Split folds at outside edges of design.

3. Place 3 rubber bands crossing in center.

4. After soaking in fixer, apply Yellow dye on 3 sections.

5. Apply Fuchsia dye on 3 sections overlapping one section of Yellow.

6. Apply Turquoise dye on one section of Fuchsia, one White section and one Yellow section. Turn shirt over and dye reverse side in same manner.

Rainbow with Black Swirl -
Fuchsia, Yellow, Turquoise and Black dye
Dye following rainbow instructions. Apply Black just to edges of folds over the Rainbow colors on the shirt.

Two-Tone Blue Swirl - Dark Blue and Turquoise dye
Dye 3 adjacent wedges Dark Blue and remaining 3 wedges Turquoise.

Graphic Swirl - Purple and Green dye
Dye 2 wedges Purple and adjacent 2 wedges Green. Leave remaining wedges White.

When you Tie-Dye you're having a good time!

These fun and easy shirts swirl and burst with a rainbow of colors. Make one in every color combination to match all your moods.

Alternating Swirl - Fuchsia, Yellow and Turquoise dye
Dye every other wedge Fuchsia then dye remaining wedges Yellow. Apply Turquoise to outside edges of folds.

TIP
Check with gloved fingers to make sure dye has penetrated down into folds. Shirt can look dyed and still have a lot of hidden White in folds.

Random Pleats

Pleated Designs can be simple, loose unbound pleats for subtle overall effect or they can be the basis for a striking multi col design. Pleating along a curved or slanted line creates an interesti variation. Draw line with pencil or disappearing ink pen, then sta pleats carefully along line.

1. Soak shirt in fixer. Place flat and arrange in 2" horizontal pleats broken in the middle.

2. Fold pleated shirt in half a place on dyeing pad. Apply Da Blue dye to edges leaving Whi areas for clouds. Dye both sid of shirt.

Blue Sky - Dark Blue dye

Pleats across the Chest

Hot Icicle - Fuchsia and Orange dye

Designing really unique shirts has never been easier. You can make almost any design your heart desires…brilliant stripes, icicles, decorative yokes, and even red, ripe watermelons.

1. Soak shirt in fixer, then arrange in vertical 2" pleats.

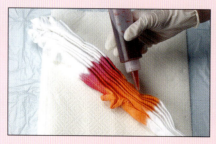

2. Apply Fuchsia and Orange dye on folds leaving rest of shirt White.

Mark dots about 4" from collar. Draw a line to connect dots. Pleat on line and place a rubber band over line and another about 3" down.

2. Apply Yellow dye and then Fuchsia dye between rubber bands. Let colors overlap. Apply Turquoise dye near collar section. Wrap Rainbow section with plastic wrap. Dye rest of shirt in a bowl with diluted Turquoise until color is smooth.

Rainbow Yoke - Fuchsia, Yellow and Turquoise dye

Watermelon Yoke - Red and Green dye, Black fabric paint, Paintbrush
Follow instructions for Rainbow collar shirt, except place second rubber band about 1" away from first rubber band. Wrap in between with plastic wrap to make a big White band. Dye yoke section Red and rest of shirt Green. After shirt is washed and dried, make 'seeds' with a fat brush and Black fabric paint.

Tri-Color Stripes - Dark Blue, Green and Purple dye
Soak shirt in fixer and arrange in vertical pleats. Bind a third of way down and two thirds of way down with several rubber bands. Dye center section Dark Blue, top a mixture of 4 parts Green and 1 part Dark Blue and bottom a mixture of 4 parts Purple and 1 part Dark Blue.

TIP: To make a wider line of White between colors, bind with 2 rubber bands about 1" apart and wrap area between rubber bands with plastic wrap.

Personalize shirts with colorful designs you stitch then dye. You'll love experimenting with different shapes, designs and color combinations.

Rainbow Heart - Turquoise, Fuchsia and Yellow dye

Stitched Designs -

In most tie-dyed designs, fabric is bound with rubber bands. However a more controlled design can be achieved using stitching. A line is drawn, stitched and gathered. If possible rubber bands are added on top of stitching to bind fabric more tightly for a distinct design. The design should be symmetric and basically round when using rubber bands. For these designs use a large eye needle and dental floss which is stronger than ordinary thread. When you apply dye, be sure to get it down into folds of bound design.

Heart Scarf - Turquoise, Fuchsia and Yellow dye
Stitch heart following instructions. Dye referring to photo.

Just what you've been waiting for!

1. Fold shirt in half lengthwise. Draw a half heart on shirt.

2. Stitch heart and pull thread to gather.

3. Place rubber band on gather line directly on top of stitching.

4. After soaking in fixer, apply Turquoise dye on heart section.

5. Apply Fuchsia dye on next section letting it overlap Turquoise to make Purple. Apply Yellow dye on next section forming large rays. Cover Rainbow section with plastic wrap. Place shirt in plastic bowl and dye rest of shirt with diluted Turquoise.

Peace Sign - Yellow and Dark Blue dye, Dinner-size plate
Place a plate on shirt, trace around it. Use a ruler to draw the lines of a peace sign. Stitch on all lines only through top layer of shirt. Wet shirt and pull up stitching evenly. Cover stitching around perimeter with several rubber bands. Insert a small cylinder into stitching so design does not buckle when bound. Soak shirt in fixer solution. Place on dyeing pad with peace sign section held away from rest of shirt. With a fine tip applicator bottle, carefully apply $\frac{1}{2}$" line of Yellow dye just on gathered lines. Apply diluted Dark Blue dye to areas inside peace sign with an applicator sponge. Cover sign section with plastic wrap. Place shirt in bowl and holding shirt up by sign section, apply diluted Blue dye to rest of shirt, rubbing dye in to make a smooth color.

lower Power - Yellow, Fuchsia and Turquoise ye, Paper for pattern, dried beans
ut a paper square. Fold in half and then thirds make 6 sections. Cut a shallow curve at center nd a deep curve on top for petals. Open pattern, ace on shirt and trace. Bind center of flower with rubber band placing beans inside to give dimen-on. Stitch around edges of flower and pull stitches ght. Bind flower line with several rubber bands. sert small bottle or cylinder inside shirt under ubber band so line does not crumple and distort esign. Dye center with Yellow mixed with a tiny bit f Fuchsia. Dye flower with half strength Fuchsia. over flower section with plastic wrap. Place shirt a bowl and holding flower section up, dye rest of hirt Lilac. To make lilac mix $\frac{1}{3}$ bottle Turquoise ith $\frac{2}{3}$ bottle of half strength Fuchsia and add 2 ottles of water.

Flower Power Fold

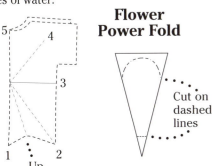

Cut on dashed lines

Resist Technique

Butterfly Scarf - Dark Blue and Turquoise dye, Paste resist, stencil, sponge
Stencil butterflies with resist and a small sponge. Remove stencil and let dry. Dye scarf with sponge and Dark Blue and Turquoise.

Valentine Cap & Socks - Fuchsia dye, Needle, Dental floss
Stitch heart in cap following instructions on page 12. Dye cap.

Rainbow Cap & Socks - Yellow, Fuchsia and Turquoise dye

4th of July Cap & Socks - Dark Blue and Red dye

What a fun and exciting way to add color to your wardrobe! Dye socks and caps for every holiday. Or just combine your favorite colors for everyday wear.

Tie-Dye Socks and Caps are a great way t add flashes of color to your wardrobe and they us very little dye. These projects are wonderful for gift and seasonal celebrations. And they are so easy to d that they are an excellent choice for group project Purchase hats at your local craft store and socks i large packages from your discount department stor Make sure hats are 100% cotton and not treated wit stain repellent. Hats with plastic visors work best. Bu socks with high cotton content. Cotton/lycra and co ton/nylon often dye better than cotton/polyester, bu any socks that have a cotton content of 80% or mor should dye well.

Crumpled Valentin Socks. Crumple soc and secure loosel with a rubber band Apply the dye wit an applicator bottle **Tip:** Stitch the hea on the cap first, refe to page 12.

Folded Rainbow Accordion fold th sock from top to bo tom, securing wit rubber bands a shown and dye eac section as desired.

Folded 4th of July Accordion fold soc bottom of sock secure with rubbe bands. Secure bean randomly in cuff. Dy bottom outside sec tions and cuff.

hristmas Cap & Socks - Green and Red dye

Folded Rainbow Hat. Fold crown of hat and secure with rubber bands. Apply dye to sections for the desired effect.

Tied Christmas Sock. Twist sock and fold in half, secure with rubber band. Dye top half Red and bottom half Green.

Tie-dye is a great community builder. Try it with your youth group or at a family reunion.

PCS = Problem - Cause - Solution

Problem - Color is too light.

Cause - The fabric is part synthetic.

Solution - Only use natural fibers. Some yardage marked cotton does not dye as brightly as it should. It may be labeled wrong or may be treated in a way that repels dye.

Cause - Dyes were not strong enough.

Solution - Add more dye. Remember that dye looks about twice as dark when first applied than after rinsed and dried. Black is the hardest. Use up to 8 tsp per 8 oz water for Black. For other dark colors, double the dye (4 tsp per 8 oz water).

Cause - Fixer solution was not used or was not strong enough.

Solution - See directions for correct dilution. Stir each time before using solution.

Cause - Dyes were not allowed to set wet on fabric long enough.

Solution - Let dye set at least 4 to 8 hours, preferably 24. Keep damp!

Cause - Dyes & water have been mixed over 2 weeks and lost potency.

Solution - Use dyes as soon as possible after mixing and keep in a cool place away from strong light.

Problem - Too much White.

Cause - Dye was not injected down into folds.

Solution - Pull folds apart with gloved fingers before you finish dyeing to check how much color is on garment. One way to avoid this problem is to dye folds first and then dye edges.

Problem - Colors are muddy and Whites are stained.

Cause - Garments not rinsed enough or crowded in washing machine.

Solution - Rinse garment more thoroughly and change water frequently. Even if you have completed washing and drying you may still be able to get excess dye out by soaking it in very hot water and washing again. Do not let dyed items sit wet on other garments because there may still be excess dye that could transfer.

Problem - Stained hands, carpet and pavement

Cause - No gloves or a hole in gloves or spilled dye.

Solution - Dye will wear off your hands in a few days and will not hurt you. Or use Reduran hand cleaner. A diluted bleach solution will remove dye from countertops and pavement and from White clothes, but be aware that it will also remove other colors. Dye washes out of polyester carpets.

Problem - Wrong color dye spots on shirt.

Cause - Touching one color on shirt with gloves that have another color on fingertips, or squirting dye out too soon.

Solution - Immediately apply water to rinse off as much as possible and reapply color you want. Or rethink design to accommodate spot. Always keep a tub of water handy to keep fingers rinsed.

Problem - Grainy, uneven color or (commonly) red 'freckles'.

Cause - Undissolved dye powders. Colors with red in them need more work.

Solution - Mix dyes with warm water that has Urea dissolved in it. If adding salt, dissolve dyes in warm water first, then add a saltwater solution. Salt inhibits dyes from dissolving. When dyeing solid colors, paste up your dye carefully as we described earlier. You can even filter it in a large funnel through some very fine fabric.

Folded Designs

Your dining room table will take on a whole new dimension when you dye napkins, bandannas, pillow tops and shirts in glowing colors. Every design will be a feast!

Tie-dye can be much more than a bright Rainbow colored T-shirt. It is an ancient craft that has been used to decorate fabrics in countries around the world for thousands of years. Interesting geometric patterns can be created by folding fabric in squares or triangles and then binding it with chopsticks and rubber bands. Clothespins can be added on some folds to make rectangular spots.

Here we show fabrics dyed with these techniques. One is called a 'flag fold' because it is based on the way a flag is folded for storage. Create a star by folding fabric into a long triangle then binding it with chopsticks at a slant.

These designs work best on light to medium weight fabric. Folds should always be done accordion style so dye will be more evenly distributed.

NOTE: The pictured designs were done on 18" square napkins.

Star Fold - Dark Blue and Turquoise dye, Chopsticks
Bind with 2 pairs of chopsticks and rubber bands. Place chopsticks on a slant to make points of star. Apply Turquoise dye to point of star and outer edges. Apply Dark Blue dye to space between chopsticks and on edges of folds.
Fold - Bring line 1 to line 2 and crease fold up on dotted line. To make second fold, bring line 2 to line 3 and crease up on dotted line. Repeat with remaining lines.

Star Fold

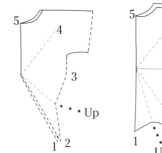
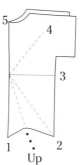

Star Fold

1. Soak napkin in fixer solution. Fold in half with right side out.

2. Mark lines on cloth wit chopsticks or a disappea ing ink pen referring to di gram above.

3. Bring lines together and fold napkin with creases up.

4. Bind with 2 pairs of chop sticks and rubber band Place chopsticks on a slan to make points of star.

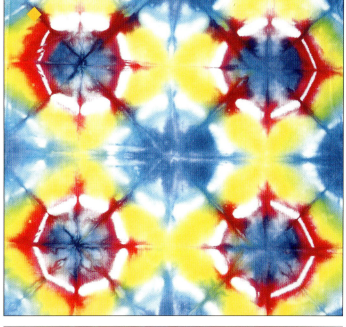

Flag Fold - Purple - Purple dye, Chopsticks, Clothespins
Flag fold and apply dye to corners.

Flag Fold - Fiesta Rainbow Colors - Dark Blue, Turquoise, Yellow and Fuchsia dye, Chopsticks, Clothespins
Apply Rainbow colors between chopsticks. Dye tips of triangle Dark Blue.

Flag Fold - Fiesta Fuchsia & Orange Colors - Fuchsia, Orange and Purple dye, Chopsticks, Clothespins
Dye tips of triangle Fuchsia. Dye area between chopsticks Orange. Apply Purple dye on edges of folds.

Flag Fold

1. Soak napkin in fixer solution. Fold napkin in half with right side in.

2. Fold one side down, turn over and fold the other side down as shown.

3. Fold into triangles, folding back and forth in an accordion style.

4. Clamp corners of triangle folds with chopsticks and rubber bands. Clamp on clothespins, using 2 clothespins in each location to accommodate thickness. Apply dye.

1. Wrap the fabric around pipe smoothly.

2. Push ends to center.

3. Secure with rubber bands.

4. Apply diagonal lines dye allowing the colors mix together.

If you have ever searched unsuccessfully for just the perfect fabrics for making home accents, you're sure to love these Shibori designs. Now you can design your own special fabrics in the colors you love.

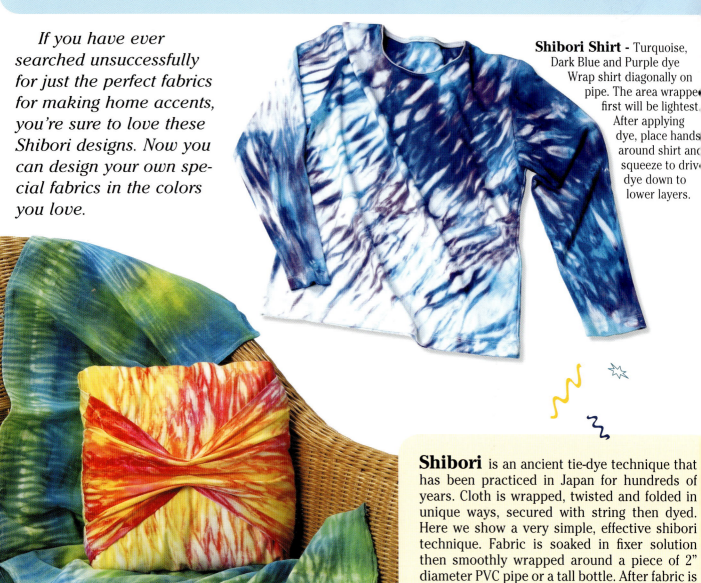

Shibori Shirt - Turquoise, Dark Blue and Purple dye Wrap shirt diagonally on pipe. The area wrapped first will be lightest. After applying dye, place hands around shirt and squeeze to drive dye down to lower layers.

Shibori is an ancient tie-dye technique that has been practiced in Japan for hundreds of years. Cloth is wrapped, twisted and folded in unique ways, secured with string then dyed. Here we show a very simple, effective shibori technique. Fabric is soaked in fixer solution then smoothly wrapped around a piece of 2" diameter PVC pipe or a tall bottle. After fabric is wrapped, ends are pushed toward center making a pattern of ripples. Place rubber bands to secure fabric. Apply dye to fabric with an applicator bottle in diagonal lines running down length of pipe. Wrap fabric with plastic wrap while it is still on the pipe to keep damp while it cures.

Shibori Curtain - Dark Blue and diluted Dark Blue dye Fold curtain lengthwise, wrap on pole diagonally and dye.

Shibori Pillow - Yellow, Fuchsia and diluted Fuchsia dye

Shibori Table Runner - Yellow, Dark Blue and Turquoise dye